THE FULL SPECTRUM
(No More Monsters!)

Yochanan Ferguson Matthews

The Full Spectrum

Spiderwize
Remus House
Coltsfoot Drive
Woodston
Peterborough
PE2 9BF

www.spiderwize.com

A CIP catalogue record for this book is available from the British Library.

Thanks to my Mother, Andy Raine, Faith Mclaine, Elisheva Ruf, and others who helped to make this book more decipherable.

1 - Introduction

This book is about harmony and diversity. Not the diversity the world talks about, devoid of the wisdom of The Maker's Instructions (Torah), a poor counterfeit rainbow. Nor the near infinite attempts of those who try to define reality using Scripture while unaware of their own personal 'bias' and limits. It is about seeing the full spectrum of The Maker's image reflected in The Body of Messiah: The Servant[1] Nation - Israel.

> The menorah of YHWH's[2] light refracted
> yet united - seven flames.

When Israel stopped listening and doing The Maker's Instructions, we were driven off, as warned, in seven directions[3], a little like at the tower of babel where speech was divided. We became a horror (zavah) to look at, a promised division (curse) while we failed to turn back wholeheartedly to following ALL[4] The Maker's instructions.

---

[1] "You are my servant, Israel, in whom I will display my splendor." Isaiah 49:3

[2] Transliterated Name of The Maker.

[3] Deuteronomy 28:25

[4] The instructions that are possible to keep while we are in exile, without the temple in Jerusalem.

Shoved by wave after wave of bitter experience
onto this sandy page,
I make my rough marks to warn and encourage.
I am unlikely to be heard,
unless The Maker of ears and hearts
opens ears and hearts to mine.
Not the best motive to write?
Beauty sours in the soul that shares not.
Yet beauty that is shared
and misjudged over and over,
is only breathing by His Promise:
That Great Expectation of a world renewed!
Holding fast till there is an end to this age of
Frankenstinian-ugliness.
That day will dawn.
His seamless body will be reborn,
clothed by the ever flowing word of life.
All creation waits.

I do not write this easily as I tried to express above. I write this with a mixture of hope and fear. In hope because The Maker has promised to turn back to us and turn us back to Beauty. Fear, because I'm tempted to project weariness onto the reader who has "heard it all before", even when they have not. Fear, because these things may seem less important to those who are "quite content with who I am, thank you" and who do not struggle with the flavour they have been made. Perhaps because they are not one of those parts of the body who regularly hear "I do not need you"[5], yet if one part suffers, every part suffers.

---

[5] 1Corinthians 12:21

There are several good teachings on this great key to wise love: Romans12. I can not compete, nor does it enter my mind to. Nor to repeat what they have done so well. I recommend their teachings[6]. Andy Raine's book "Given for life" is more like a gentle introduction when compared with Arthur Burk's series of teachings and Jackson Snyder's numerous diagnostic tools, websites and books. Jackson Snyder also sees that we should all, both houses of Israel, follow The Maker's instructions. Both Arthur and Jackson identify as the first on the Romans12 list of seven and their studies have been a little intimidating for me at times. Andy writes as one who is fourth of the seven. I'm one of the seventh on the list. How much our Romans12-flavour affects how we teach and what we focus on is worth being aware of. I have found the others helpful. They all dismiss the idea that we can be more than one at the core[7] of who we are, though we all branch out from that single trunk. For more details of this, I suggest reading the other material I have recommended.

What can I add to this subject? To affirm the setting of this wisdom with Israel's restoration: Romans chapters 8-11. To stress the need for humility if we are to see The Beauty of The Maker in the land of the living. To perhaps help point to where there are some blocks in understanding the tensions and differences in a time where some are elevated unhealthily and some under-heard or valued. I trust that there is strength and advantage in understanding some of my personal bias and limitation, my personal "plank in the eye" as a seventh of the seven.

---

[6] see appendix, I do not agree with everything and encourage wise caution

[7] Romans 12:3 - Distributed. Different - stressed in verses 4&6

All of the recommended teachings above agree that this list is "given for life"[8], i.e one of the seven is given to each, from your very beginning. To me these gifts which were 'unrepentantly given' are self evident. Sometimes *in your face*, yet sometimes beyond perception. Some who do not want to undervalue "second birth" or being "born-again", find it hard to accept this. It is true that each flavour finds its true place in the body of messiah and is ignited in a new way 'on entry' into Messiah Yeshua. To deny this pre-born-again gift is to undervalue the motivational flame given to do good, no matter how twisted it may have become before the person becomes a "believer". It also leads to a denial of the limitation The Maker has placed on each one of us, which is to teach us interdependence and therefore humility. Perhaps even to limit the damage? No place for "I'm all of them".

The two main mistakes made are to deny these single core gifts and to narrow them down / distort them.

It is critical to understand the difference between the three lists[9] in Paul's writings. Simply put they are: Tools[10] we may each use, Jobs[11] we may have for a time and the Romans12 gifts of "Who we are" (or the "why you do what you do", motivational flavour). These are important differences because people tend to get caught up with big tools or the value placed on a job, on function rather than the joy of just being.

---

[8] The name of Andy Raine's book about Romans12.

[9] 1 Corinthians 12:4-7 Tools, Jobs, Motivations

[10] 1 Corinthians 12:7 +

[11] Ephesians 4

The survival mind is preoccupied with skills which will be useless when the earth is restored. Narrowed down by fear, the functions distort the image of The Maker, exaggerating some and shrinking others. Some less obviously "useful" types are judged to be useless against The Maker's design.

At best Romans 12, perfectly placed in Paul's letter, can clear the way to let The Maker reveal himself once again and therefore His Kingdom come.

I trust that this will provoke thought and discussion.

Let the beauty of The Maker be upon us.[12]

---

[12] Psalm 90:17

2 - Setting the pearl (Romans chapter 12) in its right fixing (Romans Chapters 8-11).

In His good wisdom, The Maker chose one nation: Israel, to be the "Firstborn"[13] nation to lead the other nations through service, a good Big Brother. A nation of priests in the order of Melchitzedek, Righteous-King. [14] This wisdom goes against the evil of ambition which is the unsurrendered will. To the modern mind it looks like elitism or even racism! This order is eternally fixed: Plan A with no plan B.

Likewise within Israel, the tribe of Levi was given a distinct role of service, and within Levi, the descendants of Aharon are set apart for an even more distinct role. Romans twelve shows this same kind of wisdom.

After being rescued from Egypt, Israel were given The Maker's Instructions which are described as life to those who receive them. [15] The sum of these instructions expresses the full nature of The Maker. While Israel heard and did what The Maker instructed: Torah, they were blessed and were the intended blessing to the other nations. This is what most of the Bible is about. While Israel is in its place as firstborn the whole world benefits and while in exile there is trouble. However they became discontent with being different from the other nations. After King David's time they stopped representing The Maker well. When his

---

[13] I recommend Ephraim Frank's book: Firstborn Factor

[14] 1Peter 2:9 Exodus 19:6

[15] Deuteronomy 30:15 -17 Torah = Life and Good

son, Solomon, overburdened Israel with un-torah-like taxes, Israel was split into two nations: Judah and Israel. In insecurity, Jeroboam, king of Israel, set up "counterfeit Jerusalems" in Dan and Beitel, a pattern seen to this day. Eventually both houses were exiled and their influence diminished, being dysfunctional or absent. The Jews (Judah and Benjamin) remained known and seen through time, while Israel (also called: 10 lost tribes of Israel, Joseph, Ephraim, Samaria, "Not my people"[16]) became 'lost' or hidden .... that is until recently!

It is also important to know that while Israel is in a time of humbling, split into two and exiled from the land, there are other "big brothers" who desire to fill the vacuum made by Israel's temporary rejection. If we stick to the biblical narrative we will see that Ishmael and Edom are the two main characters who have **not** yet come to terms with **not** being chosen for this role of Firstborn. If we don't stick to the narrative we will project onto biblical prophecies all manner of science-fiction ideas such as the popular George Orwell '1984' conspiracy.

When thinking of The Kingdom of The Maker, think: King David. Until recently the message of personal salvation has monopolised what is thought of as "The Gospel", creating a spiritualised etherial kingdom. All this because of not understanding the unchanging plan to have Israel the nation, chosen for leadership over the other nations. Most of scripture is about our National salvation. Much individualism and confusion has flooded in. Instead: "Your Kingdom come, Your will be done on **earth** as it is in the heavens".

---

[16] Hosea chapter 1

No nation replaces Israel permanently. As Daniel chapter two explains, only five nations / empires / kingdoms fill the vacuum while the set time of rejection for Israel completes itself. Even longer for Northern Israel: 2730 years![17][18] Paul is writing mainly to those coming back to their Israelite identity again, not to Jews who did not lose theirs. He is talking to us today who have reached the end of the promised 2730 years rejection. Restored Israel, both houses / sticks / nations, both Judah and Ephraim, together they have the role as Firstborn Leadership Nation, shown in servanthood. The "not my people"[19] becoming again "sons of The Maker"[20] The letter of Romans chapters 8-11 covers the reunification of the two houses of Israel becoming one flock, one stick in Ezekiel 34:23 & 37:22 and all over Scripture.

Now is the time of the end of the long rejection of Israel. Time for the two sticks to be joined together[21] to fulfil their servant position as Firstborn. This generation gets to see the restored order of The Maker that brings peace on earth; The Great Shabbat[22]. Now that's good news!

All this is the context Paul gives us in chapters 1 to 11, leading us into the next chapter, 12, which welcomes us into that Pearl of Beauty-Pleasantness: the seven branched menorah of people. This is the firm foundation which fixes this gem into its proper setting where we find our true place together in the body, Israel, reflector of YHWH's likeness.

---

[17] Ezekiel chapter 4, two different times of exile for Judah and Israel

[18] Leviticus 26:18

[19] Hosea 1 / Romans 9:25-26 / 1Peter 2:10

[20] Hosea 1 / Romans 9:25-26 / 1Peter 2:10

[21] Ezekiel 37:19 -22 two sticks

[22] 7th thousand years, Sabbath day of 1000years

Without this foundation, the unity gained would be another counterfeit Big Brother, a tower of babel ambition. Coming together outside of the Firstborn plan, may create unity but it is doomed to failure and ugliness.

"Remember the Torah of Moses my servant, which I commanded him in Horeb for <u>all</u> Israel, *with* the statutes and judgments. Behold, I will send you EliYah the prophet before the coming of the great and dreadful day of the YHWH: And he shall turn the heart of the fathers to the children, and the heart of the children to their fathers, lest I come and strike the earth with a curse" Malachi 4: 4,5,6

(As when Israel left Egypt in the exodus it will be the same in the <u>second greater exodus</u>[23] when there will be a multitude who will join them.)

---

[23] The "rapture" idea comes from the first exodus. See Appendix notes on The Greater Exodus

3 - A brief introduction to the magnificent seven.

"For You formed my inward parts; You knit me together in my mother's womb. I will praise You, for I am fearfully and wonderfully made; Marvellous are Your works, and that my soul knows very well. My frame was not hidden from You, when I was made in secret, and skilfully wrought in the lowest parts of the earth. Your eyes saw my substance, being yet unformed. And in Your book they all were written, the days fashioned for me, when as yet there were none of them. Psalm 139:13-16

Romans chapter twelve is not the list of tools that we may each use as believers listed in the first letter to Corinthians chapter12[24]. Neither is it the list of jobs described in the letter to Ephesians chapter 4. It is a list of 'who you are' or the 'why you do something', rather than just what you do. Seven gifts that people are motivated by of differing attributes or strengths of The Maker. They are our seven favours, gifts, advantages, colours, textures, vantage points or flavours. They stem from beyond the world of action in the realm of motivation and being.

It is critical to understand the difference between the three lists in Paul's writings because people tend to get caught up in the value placed on a job, or function rather than the joy of just being. The survival world is preoccupied with skills which will be useless when the earth is restored. Narrowed down by fear, those functions which are perceived as more valuable will inevitably distort the image of The Maker.

---

[24] 1 Corinthians 12:4-7 Tools, Jobs, Motivations

"**Power Tools**" - In 1 Corinthians 12 they are called
<u>pneumatikoi</u>, or "spirituals" (an adjective, modifying an
implied noun such as "things"). "Spiritualities" might be a
good literal rendering. We call them "numatics" these are
received through obedience, belief and asking. Called
"*Diversities of operations" in 1* Corinthians 12:6.

"**Jobs**" - In Ephesians 4 and 1 Corinthians 12:28 they are
<u>domata</u>, primarily translated as "gifts" but perhaps more
accurately as "grantings" – these are "callings" on the lives
of certain people, gifts of people to a congregation. or
"*Differences of administrations" in*
1 Corinthians 12:5.

"**Flavours**" - In Romans 12, Paul calls this "gifts" list
<u>charismata</u>, literally "graces" – inborn and switched on more
fully at spiritual birth. They are also explained as
"motivational gifts" and "*Diversities of gifts" in 1* Corinthians
12:4. Jackson Snyder prefers to call them Favours, because
gifts carries the idea that we choose to receive them. These
are what this book is about.

The seven flavours.

I like to refer to them as flavours or by the number they are
ordered in; 1 to 7. Flavour seems to help capture for me the
essence of inborn diversity. That is my preference and
therefore I refer to them mostly that way in this book. If it is
helpful for you, good. If not, please replace it with the word
you think best fits what Paul is teaching us about.

After some introductory wisdom to all (Romans 12:1-5), the
passage is then broken down into; 1/ a list of the seven gifts
(Romans 12:6-8), then 2/ these seven listed with their
purpose or focus; their potential strengths (Romans 12:9-
15), then finally 3/ the seven are listed with warnings of their

potential misuses / weaknesses needing to be covered by the other six (12:16-21). Until explained this way, the verses following the seven gifts listed(1) look like a long stream of general advice (verses 9-21). I trust it will become obvious to you if not already, that the twelve verses following them is wise advice directly related to each of the "favoured flavours"[25]. I have used colour below to connect the gift with the relevant wisdom.

1/Romans 12:6-8 The List
If your gift is prophesying, then prophesy in to the level of your trust.
If it is serving, then serve.
If it is teaching, then teach.
If it is to encourage, then give encouragement.
If it is giving, then give generously.
If it is to lead, do it diligently.
If it is to show mercy, do it cheerfully.

2/Romans 12:9-15 Potential strengths to develop.
Love must be sincere. Hate what is evil; cling to what is good.
Be devoted to one another in love. Honour one another above yourselves.
Never be lacking in zeal, but keep your spiritual fervour, serving The Maker.
Be joyful in hope, patient in affliction, faithful in prayer.
Share with The Maker's people who are in need. Practice hospitality.
Bless those who persecute you; bless and do not curse.

---

[25] a Jackson Snyder term

Rejoice with those who rejoice; mourn with those who mourn.

3/Romans 12:16-21 Potential inherent weaknesses to overcome.
Live in harmony with one another.
Do not be proud, but be willing to associate with people of low position.
Do not be conceited.
Do not repay anyone evil for evil.
Be careful to do what is right in the eyes of everyone.
If it is possible, as far as it depends on you, live at peace with everyone.
Do not take revenge, my dear friends, but leave room for The Maker's wrath, for it is written: "It is mine to avenge; I will repay," says The Maker.
On the contrary: "If your enemy is hungry, feed him; if he is thirsty, give him something to drink. In doing this, you will heap burning coals on his head."
Do not be overcome by evil, but overcome evil with good.

(sorry if I chose colours that you don't think suit your flavour!)

Gift name, Gift strengths to develop, Gift potential weakness.

It is foundational to understanding this message that these gifts were given long before the "born-again" experience. From conception at least. It goes against the grain for many due to poor teaching. The alternative is unthinkable yet widely accepted sadly. Despising the pre-new-birth gifting is part of the problem, denying the very need for healing or reordering. Rightly these gifts were given to be active in The Body of Messiah (read:Israel). Surrendered to The Maker but given none the less, generously to all. I have written these descriptions mainly for believers but it can be very helpful for people who do not yet believe, to talk about their flavour.

Seven types compared to parts of the body, these teach dependency for unity (Beauty and Pleasantness). He has not put all of His abilities / attributes into each of us but spread them out. For as we have many members in one body, and all members have not the same "function"… (Please let me remind you these are not Paul's list of Jobs).

Love one another: The full spectrum of love.

1/ Prophet. ~ (note: not the job of prophet in Ephesians 4 or the tool of prophecy) Proclaim Truth. Strong flavoured; haters of evil, lovers of good. Black and White. Radical and restless. Inspirational. Their sharp minds have the ability to discern people's motives like lightning. They identify, define, and hate evil, and speak to injustice. They are direct, frank, and powerfully persuasive when speaking. With their strong voice they often lead. Their style of leadership is "I'm off, who's coming?" and they will often leave others to finish projects they have started. The motivational prophet is someone who likes to discover The Maker's principles, analyze them and use them to solve problems. They make known the thoughts of The Maker on grounds of His principles. They are task orientated rather than people or relationship-orientated, yet emotional. They are quick verbally. They seek evidence of change that someone has turned from wrong. They may like to be told their own 'blind spots', places where they are 'missing it'. They are visionaries who can see far ahead to consequences. They need to have a dream.

The prophets' weaknesses include: intimidation, lack of compromise, negativity, not people-oriented, depressed. They must not get their legitimacy from their ability to solve problems. They can enjoy causing trouble especially when bored, hence the warning to live in harmony (verse16). While they can discern peoples' motives they can, in their speed, also get them wrong. The hard Prophet is balanced by the soft Mercy on the other extreme end of the menorah. Prophet flavoured people need to work actively on building and maintaining relationships with people. They have to learn that unless you have relationship with someone, you mostly do not have the right to speak into that person's life. Naturally abrupt and blunt they therefore often seem to be insensitive to other people's feelings. They tend to be intolerant, critical and condemning of those who are not like them. When they do not embrace Romans 12 diversity they may look down on others, "they do not suffer fools gladly", it can be a negative thing. They may often be too interested in groups and forget the individual. They like to see dramatic change and don't naturally approve of people changing gradually.

2/ Server. ~ These people are practical and ingenious. Good with things. Often seen on the go. They see needs and meet them quickly. They have great stamina, and will work extra hard to complete a task, enjoying short-range goals. They need appreciation and opportunity to serve others. The servant is designed to create an atmosphere and a environment where the King of kings is welcome and feels comfortable. They are task-orientated yet fulfilling tasks with the aim of helping people. They are rarely verbally or emotionally expressive. They are often the ones who clean or make sure chairs are ready for a meeting, but it is important not to see the servant only in this way. This gift has great authority to clean the spiritual atmosphere through warfare and to rearrange and sustain life on many levels. They know the likes and dislikes of others. Servants see easily what needs to be done and then do what is necessary to meet that need. They are essential armour bearers to leadership, providing a safe place / atmosphere where others can recuperate when they come in from the battlefield. They require detailed explanation of how to do the task if they don't already know how to do it. They are happy when others are pleased with their work. They need sincere appreciation of the work done. They are intercessors as they can often see what needs to be prayed for. They serve often at great cost to themselves and their families. They focus on leading through service.

The servants' weaknesses include: difficulty in being served, seen wrongly as unspiritual, in danger of being exploited by groups. "Do not be proud, but be willing to associate with people of low position". They struggle to say no and to set healthy borders for what they are capable of doing in a set time period. This causes them to be misused and overworked, often to the detriment of their own families. Servants do not easily verbalise their emotions although they do influence the atmosphere with them. They like to have their feet on the ground and can resist being out of their emotional depth. Once they are challenge out of their depth, they can be stretch to be able to manage more change. They tend to become disgusted with those who are insensitive to other people's needs. They appear to be pushy and push others out of their jobs. They may contribute to others' irresponsibility and laziness by doing too much for them when there is no real need. Their desire to help can interfere with The Maker's plans.

3/ Teacher. ~ They may not be a school-teacher or lecturer or writer or researcher as their job. Someone training for any one of those jobs may have to be taught priorities or skills that come naturally to someone with a teaching motivation. As happens with the prophet flavoured people, Teachers are not to confused with the job of Teaching listed in Ephesians 4. Anyone may be called to that job (ministry) regardless of their Romans 12 flavour.

They are an explainer. Summarise large amounts of information very concisely. Clarifiers of truth. They are ponderers and chewers. Thoughtful. They have amazing memories for facts and details. Teachers love to research words and validate truth, or compare what is generally thought to be true or right with the Bible or any field of knowledge. Even when teaching flavoured people are not able to read or are not adept at putting words down on paper, they would be recognisable as teachers, deliberate, thoughtful, interested to learn, respectful of experts in any field. Teachers who are believers, are uncomfortable with anything that cannot be proven in the Bible. They take lots of time to make decisions and hate to be rushed. They are verbally expressive and emotionally stable. They passionately share their knowledge with others on subjects that interest them. They love to do research and will seek answers for any question on those subjects. They either invent or are often the catalyst for invention. They quote the Bible in context. They need to know who is the source of information / teaching. They tend to accept new ideas and teachings slowly, taking their time to make sure. The fact that the teacher flavour moves slower than the other gifts, protects the community from taking action based on false leads and also gives the wayward time to return to the path. Guardians of established truth. They enjoy analyzing facts – have an analytical mind. They test the knowledge of those who teach, asking if it is Scriptural. They are concerned with proofs and logical thought processes. Enjoy solving problems – is a thinker. They may be reluctant to accept new ideas and concepts unless they can be thoroughly substantiated. They love to teach with Scriptural illustrations.

Teachers' weaknesses include the seeming appearance of lacking warmth because of being so analytical. They can lack practical application of Scripture or in the rest of life, in favour of more academic research, tending to shut themselves up in an "ivory tower" of theory, and to lose touch with reality. The acquisition of knowledge can become an end in itself, rather than a means to an end. Ironically these can become very sentimental and nostalgic. Their warning is not be conceited as they can become proud of or controlling of their knowledge. They may easily be contemptuous of new ideas (or lost old ones!) and opinions. They become frustrated with those who do not think as logically as they do, and those who do not see as much need for proofs. Teachers can fall into traditional belief and legalism if they do not focus on having a personal and intimate relationship with The Maker. It is The Presence of The Maker who keeps the truth alive. They may become boring with their sharing of technical data in too much detail. Sometimes they tolerate false teaching – not submitting to it – but not confronting it either.

4/ Exhorter. ~ Encourager or Motivator[26] Stimulators of the trust of others. People-focused in whatever quantity. Positive. "Joyful in hope, patient in affliction, faithful in prayer" People of faith. Able to see both sides of the

---

[26] This gift & the organiser, can be seen in two forms according to Jackson Snyder p76 "Spiritual Gifts Revelation"

argument being in the middle of the menorah[27]. They desire to help people improve themselves, providing practical steps. Natural counsellors. They want practical applications that apply to life, not just information. The exhorter is verbally as well as emotionally expressive, and relationship-focused. They build networks of relationships with the purpose of building community. They often have relationships with people across the social borders of congregation, race and the wider community. They have a keen sense of the processes and seasons necessary to bring about changes that will reach a goal or vision. Exhorters have no problem seeing how suffering might help produce maturity, (but it seems less easily in themselves!). Some exhorters would prefer to offer criticism only very rarely, and instead to always look for the potential in an individual or situation. Others would offer criticism as the very thing that could enable someone to address their problems and move on to achieve their potential. They need the acceptance of others. They love to see their advice being used to meet needs, and often document their successes. They are soft on the outside, however, they are able to be ruthless in achieving their goals.

The exhorters' weaknesses are in being too quick to compromise. As they favour keeping the harmony in the group relationships, they compromise on strict guidelines given from Above. They can be prone to "wallpapering over the cracks" to keep the feeling of unity. The exhorters' families may suffer as they often try to fit just *one more* person or appointment or job into a minute. They seem to have short attention spans because they need to see the practical application of a message quickly. They can abuse

---

[27] That is if each flavour is one of the seven-light-menorah in Romans 12 order.

their power to push themselves on others' will to achieve their goals rather than to motivate and encourage. They are in danger of spending too much time on relationships with people and too little time on their relationship with The Maker. Conflict and tension in relationships can feel life-threatening to them. They can be over-lavish in his praise and compliments until the value of their praise can be undermined. They need to receive The Maker's wisdom in place of their own natural wisdom.

5/ Giver. ~ These are deep and mysterious. They are generous with money and their time. They make wise purchases and good investments. They are *industrious* – hard workers; they have an ability to make money. They give without desiring to be known. They often see needs that others overlook, and anonymously meet the need. Givers are joyful when they find their gifts to be answers to prayer, supernatural timing. Since their gifts are high quality, they desire to be a part of the work to which they are giving. They are very accommodating of different opinions so are able to be the glue that keeps very different people together. They have a long term vision of provision for others and the next generation. They save, look for the best value for money, and see business and other opportunities that others do not see. Givers often live in a very frugal fashion, seemingly not interested in meeting their families' needs. They are not naïve, and they quickly see and discern false motives and manipulation. They depend easily on The Maker to meet their financial need. They are wise in their giving. They are independent people who look after themselves and others. Have an intercessory role in the body of Messiah.

Weaknesses of the giver include: They need protecting from over-extending themselves as they may not be able to see when or say, "Enough is enough". They are project - rather than people-orientation, therefore they are judgmental about how others use their money and materials. They appear to want to control, and seem mean when they do not respond to a need. They may be stingy and gather possessions out of fear. Their independence can be a stumbling block as they need to accept dependence on The Maker for salvation and provision. They can focus on meeting physical needs only. Often desiring to control the work they give to, trying to control how contributions are used. Sometimes they fail to obey The Maker's prompting immediately as they can be too secure in their independence.

6/ Organiser. ~ (Ruler, Coordinators, Administrator): These are good organisers, able to see the final picture, and clarify long-range goals. They are able to analyze a situation quickly and make a judgment or a decision – and it is usually the right one. They are not procrastinators, but want to get the job done as expediently as possible. They make tough decisions that people may never know about. They are networkers, aware of resources, and do not push for leadership positions. They are willing to endure negative reactions from other workers if the job is getting done. They are able to coordinate the efforts of many people at once. They are often chosen for leadership. They are loyal and expect loyalty. Organisers are energetic, verbally expressive, task orientated and controlled emotionally. They are motivated when leading and are passionate about administrating and implementing the tasks necessary to complete projects. They have the ability to build empires, starting with only a few resources. The end goal is important. They are not perfectionists, only focused on "does it work or not?" They like to work with people and have the ability to motivate. They manage time and priorities well. They have respect for authority and submit easily to it, and expect the same from those they are appointed over. They delegate authority easily and with success. They do not offer to do something – they expect tasks to be delegated to them. For them, offering help often means that they are transgressing on someone else's area of authority. Once a task is delegated to them they will take responsibility for it and do it right the first time. Giving them responsibility for a task without delegating the appropriate authority to implement the task paralyses them to such an extent that they would rather withdraw from the task. They are excellent implementers. Not a fault of their own, but because they are fast thinkers, and also they think of every thing, others are overwhelmed by their gift, and so Organisers very often are envied.

The Organiser must leave revenge in The Maker's hands. Their weaknesses include dependence on the plan instead of The Maker. Being so private with their emotions does not mean they do not have any. The Organiser's ability to build empires can become a stumbling block for living in dependency on The Maker. Their ability to delegate can appear to be laziness. Their ability to endure reactions of others may appear to be callousness. They often do not explain their plans, and seem insensitive to others, making them feel used. They may tend to view people as resources rather than individuals. As a result of regular criticism of being controlling, Organisers can build walls around themselves and become even more task orientated and absent from the team. They then start either to work on their own or they become like slave masters. They may become workaholics as this may become a way of escaping the pain of relationships and emotional involvement. Reaching the goal no matter what becomes their focus. They may show favouritism or partiality to those they consider more important to achieving goals. They may be reluctant to dismiss valuable workers with serious issues. They may be in danger of causing rebellion by being critical of leaders above them.

7/ Mercy. ~ (Empath) Laughs with those who laugh, cries with those who cry, therefore changes from person to person. An Empath is not the same as someone being sympathetic or even empathetic, as it is much less to do with choice. They can not choose whether or not to feel people's and group's emotions and atmospheres. They are soft and can not easily hide their emotions. People focused, much preferring one to one. They hope to remove the hurts of others, and are sensitive to words and deeds that can hurt. They are naturally tolerant and liberal. They forgive easily, once they know / accept that they have been sinned against. 'Sinners' feel accepted by these people easily. They tend to spend most time with the 'outsider', the hurting, the bereaved or the most vulnerable. They are more concerned for where someone is at, emotionally / mentally, rather than for physical needs. They have an intrinsic design for seeking The Maker's perfect and complete Kingdom, nothing less will do. People with the mercy flavour are naturally emotionally expressive and are normally less verbally expressive. They can enter into The Maker's presence easily and can help others to do so. As they are open emotionally they are easy to trust. They can sense when something is wrong but will probably not be able to explain how they know. Opposites attract, they love the clear voice of the prophet. They rarely have enemies. They can often be father or mother figures to others. They do not like those who they perceive to be insensitive or hurtful. They react to those who are insensitive to the feelings of others. They do not defend themselves easily but become angry on behalf of others. Their desire for perfection is often criticised as perfectionism by others with the result that they may leave an organisation or a congregation and if they stay they may settle for mediocrity.

The weaknesses of the Mercy include being easily wounded. All these changes of emotion from person to person, especially in groups, can be extremely tiring for them. Therefore they need much physical distance and time to recover and process it all. Sometimes they don't see when to hold back with mercy to let the suffering for sin *do its work*; to help the person hunger for change. In which case they need to be certain sin is the reason for the suffering. Physical touch is important to them and their affectionate nature is easily misinterpreted as sexual attraction or interest. They are gullible and vulnerable to being pushed into unwanted or unhealthy sexual relations. Their need for much physical touch may lead them to compromise and accept relationships that are not healthy or right. They are vulnerable to being used and abused and therefore need lots of support to escape the victim mentality. They do not want to be much trouble but can end up monopolising time and attention inappropriately. They may have to wait until a more appropriate time, even if the emotions have already spilled up and over. If a mercy has been deeply hurt and betrayed by others, they will forgive easily but find it very difficult to find a good reason for exposing themselves to the same threat. They struggle to make decisions if someone is going to be hurt in the process. They tend to avoid giving discipline when in a leadership position and with parenting. Their avoidance of firmness may appear as weakness. They do not function well under pressure, they pressure themselves enough. If they delay making decisions, more events requiring action build up and they end up in inertia. They tend to avoid confronting wrong behaviour. Their distancing of themselves from an individual or group, may appear as cowardice but can be the only way they see of keeping the unity. As they can't hide emotions, they can sometimes be found hiding behind the "washing up" for safety in group settings. Overwhelmed easily with evil, they must learn to overcome evil with good through simple trust in the goodness of The Maker. In a place of being overwhelmed they find it very hard to get on with everyday disciplines. If they fail to overcome evil with good they tend to become mediocre or lukewarm[28], settling for the status quo, letting the The Maker down. Men with this gift are often traditionally perceived as not "male" enough for a man's world, yet The Maker created this gift so perception has to change. These may be the most likely of all the seven to confess to 'crimes' they have not committed.

——— ——— ———

These suggestions are to help affirm and position your personal flavour when you recognise it. They are not to narrow you down or box you wrongly. The opposite is true, when received in the right way much personal freedom is gained from trying "to change the things I can't" and to find "courage to change the things I can". It is much wisdom to know the difference.

Some find it easy to recognise which one they are, despite having other flavoured branches as well. Some do not. "The person inside may be hidden or squashed or damaged, but is still there".[29] It is sometimes the irritating things others do that can help you discover your flavour.

---

[28] Revelation 3:16
[29] p86 "Given For Life" Andy Raine

Other differences, such as gender or culture will also be part of your story.

Once again, I suggest reading Andy Raine's book for his flavour's perspective and way of teaching about this diversity. Also Arthur Burk's dvd series which goes so much deeper than I have here. Some people see which flavour they are at the core quickly, for others it takes more time. In Andy Raine's book, "Given For Life", he goes through 'tie-breakers' for those who are not yet sure between two or three out of the seven. Jackson Snyder goes much deeper, seeking to unmask souls from survival behaviour where their gifts were not affirmed or were even despised. Sometimes a parent's flavour is the most evident. Sometimes people have been unconsciously trying to be like the flavours they think are more 'cool' (attractive, prestigious) or desirable. For those who have had affirmation for their flavour there may be other issues. All will need to begin to recognise where the tensions are in their relationships with the other flavours. Either insecurities or prejudices which, in this light are able to be worked on by The Maker, not to remove the necessary tension, but to bring harmony - True Shalom[30].

It happens that a person identifies clearly as one of the seven with little doubt, only later to realise they were mistaken. This is usually because one or both parents were unable to affirm the gifting in a fairly serious way and the child seeking to please the parent developed by mirroring the parent's gifting. Removing these "mask" giftings and accepting the core flavour is such a fruitful, though painful, process. Jackson Snyder has a series of tools to help separate parental influence from the core flavour. There are

---

[30] competition (peace)

others who can not work out which one of two or three motivations they are. There is no rush, and there can be several reasons why it is not yet clear. The Maker will reveal it and bring harmony in His good time.

Gender is an important related topic. Some flavours can be seen as more masculine and some more feminine, though in various cultures this can differ. This revelation can bring much healing and acceptance, once seen.

There are many sevens in scripture. The order of their appearance matches the order in Romans12, it seems: days of the week, Mishcan (tabernacle) 'furniture', feasts or annual meeting times, trees, names of The Maker, fruits of promise, congregations in the Book of Revelation...and more.

~There are seven people at the table, each one is a different flavour and they have just finished their main course. In come the desserts on a tray but they don't make it to the table. The beautiful dessert is on the floor.
The Prophet flavoured: "That's what happens when you're not careful!"
The Server gets up and helps.
The Teacher thinks about it all, then explains "the custard jar was far heavier than the bowls and was over one side making the tray imbalanced"
The Encourager says "Next time let's serve the dessert with the meal. (correcting the future)
The Giver goes off to get another dessert quickly.
The Organiser says "Jim get the mop, Sue please help pick up broken glass, Mary would you get some newspaper to

wrap the glass in, I'll get some more bowls ready for when Sheila gets back with the new dessert"

The Mercy says "Ohh..Never mind! ...... I did just the same thing round at Michael's!"

~Fred is in hospital and gets seven visitors, each one is a different flavour!

The Prophet asks if Fred can see what The Maker is trying to say to him through this situation. Is there something to put right?

The Server brings the mail, a little gift, and reassures Fred that he has watered his plants and fed the cat.

The Teacher says "I did some research on your illness and I believe I can explain what's happening"

The Encourager comes in and says "How can we use what you're learning here to help others in the future?"

The Giver says "Are you going to be in difficulty financially with being off work so long? or is that all taken care of?"

The Organiser says "Don't worry about a thing. I've assigned your job to four others in the office"

The Mercy says "I can't begin to tell you how I felt when I found out that you were sick. How do you feel now?"

~What sort of Chocolate are you?

Mercies and Givers are the soft centred (Givers are much less easily recognisable as soft. They are mysterious).

Prophets are hard, strong tasting.

Servers are also firm, hard centres, but less likely to break your teeth.

Teachers are chewy centres.

Encouragers look soft, liquid surface, but are hard underneath.

Rulers appear to be the hardest of them all but have liqueur centres inside.

~

Character is maturity and is not inborn, unlike these flavoured advantages.

This is really only a taster and I recommend going deeper with the help of those I have recommended already (see appendix). The next chapter is an attempt to name some blocks, to the body functioning well and being beautiful. It focuses on man-made disasters, the negative to be removed, to let The Maker's image be seen in fullness. Therefore please approach the next chapter with caution and even put the book down if The Maker wants to talk to you about your flavour. It is not my motivation to overwhelm you with some of the problems as I perceive them. If possible read "Given for life" first. If not take it in bite-size pieces. I am sensitive to this as a "Number 7": "Do not become overwhelmed with evil, but overcome evil with good"[31]

I trust you can see that what Paul is opening up to us is something none of us have seen fully here on earth, except

---

[31] Romans 12:21

perhaps in heavenly vision. It is the restoration of The Name of The Maker:

The Full Spectrum.

4 - The Bad News

When I'm asked if I want the good news or the bad news first, I always ask for the bad news so I can get it out of the way. So here's the bad news: you are ugly!

"The Maker will cause you to be defeated before your enemies. You will come at them from one direction but flee from them in seven, and you will become a thing of horror[32] to all the kingdoms on earth." Deuteronomy 28:25

"You will become a thing of horror[33], a byword and an object of ridicule among all the peoples where The Maker will drive you. "Deuteronomy 28:37

We are a horror! But some will say "In Jesus we are forgiven", meaning all those curses are all gone. Are they yet? We are still sick. We are often divided and fearful. We are still mostly divided into two nations. We are still mostly in exile, scattered. The ultimate curse was to be told "you are not my people"[34] and we were sent off into a deep exile with a loss of identity. Zealous to be faithful to what Messiah has done for us, many teach all the curses are gone. It is a form of corporate denial. A denial of the bad news and therefore not open to the full good news. Do not lose heart. The

---

[32] zavah - moved, shaken,horror

[33] shamah - a waste, a horror, an appalling thing

[34] Hosea chapter 1 see also Romans 9:25-26 / 1Peter 2:10 House of Israel not Judah.

Maker has promised to end all these curses. So He will. In Deuteronomy chapter 30, He promises our return to His land and re-acceptance as His people and with a fresh heart to hear and do all His instructions[35]. A greater second exodus and return Home and to be One[36]. Because of Yeshua's complete work we can taste right now a wonderful deposit of what is to come.

Paul reveals the two sides we fall off the path:
"Even so the body is not made up of one part but of many. Now if the foot should say, "Because I am not a hand, I do not belong to the body," it would not for that reason stop being part of the body. And if the ear should say, "Because I am not an eye, I do not belong to the body," it would not for that reason stop being part of the body. If the whole body were an eye, where would the sense of hearing be? If the whole body were an ear, where would the sense of smell be? But in fact The Maker has placed the parts in the body, every one of them, just as he wanted them to be. If they were all one part, where would the body be? As it is, there are many parts, but one body. The eye cannot say to the hand, "I don't need you!" And the head cannot say to the feet, "I don't need you!" On the contrary, those parts of the body that seem to be weaker are indispensable,and the parts that we think are less honourable we treat with special honour. And the parts that are unpresentable are treated with special modesty, while our presentable parts need no special treatment. But The Maker has put the body together, giving greater honour to the parts that lacked it, so that there should be no division in the body, but that its parts should have equal concern for each other. If **one part**

---

[35] This is the "new covenant" or "new testament" - or renewed covenant.
[36] John 17:21

36

suffers, every part suffers with it; if one part is honoured, every part rejoices with it. Now you are the body of Messiah, and each one of you is a part of it." 1Corinthians 12:14-28[37].

Two errors: The "I don't belong" or The "You don't belong"

Isaiah 11

Talking about bad news, let's go back to the very beginning, it's a very <u>Good</u> place to start. Those who are not open to the bad news of "The Fall": the entrance of death, sickness and suffering for the first time, caused by not following The Maker's instructions, into the freshly made world, will not be open to the good news of the world's restoration. It is perhaps understandable when a denyer of The Maker, with their alternative story of origins, believes the above naturalism, but it is much harder to understand people who call themselves believers who talk of millions of years of death being part of an intelligent "creation". In denial of this bad news they are not open to The Good News of Isaiah chapter eleven. Those who don't 'get' that "death is not normal or natural" will not be able to grasp the bad news I'm trying to highlight in this chapter.

The true Norm is:

"The wolf will live with the lamb, the leopard will lie down with the goat, the calf and the lion and the yearling together; and a little child will lead them. The cow will feed with the

---

[37] Here Paul is using this metaphor with other differences (Isaiah 11:13), however he uses the body metaphor in Romans 12 also.

bear, their young will lie down together, and the lion will eat straw like the ox. The infant will play near the cobra's den, and the young child will put its hand into the viper's nest. They will neither harm nor destroy on all my holy mountain, for the earth will be filled with the knowledge of The Maker as the waters cover the sea." Isaiah 11:6 - 9

Ironically this cynical generation that mocks Isaiah 11's Happy Origin and Happy Ending as foolishness, enforces multiculturalism; the predator and prey of the Isaiah chapter 11 scenario are forced to live together peaceably.[38] This expectation is premature and foolish.

It is easy to see how an atmosphere of fear could cause the "stronger" gifts to appear more important. Those who sound confident and clear will lead. Those who prevaricate naturally or who are not quick to find words to explain what they see, may be sidelined. For all sorts of reasons patterns of discrimination will develop. These then continue into longer lasting and ingrained traditions. None of these are according to The Maker's design and therefore not healthy, let alone beautiful. So a spirit of survival shapes the community. The status quo: "That's life!" No! Survival is not fullness of life! Isaiah 11[39] is.

If we say we love Him but say to other parts of the body "I do not need you"……

---

[38] An example: Euro-Arab Dialogue. Barcelona Process 1995

[39] also includes the reunion of both houses: Judah and Ephraim

In this cursed creation there are some who tend to be more predator-like and some more prey-like. Romans 12 joins with Isaiah 11 as the vision of restoration of unity and beauty.

"Some of them want to use you. Some of them want to get used by you. Some of them want to abuse you. Some of them want to be abused" [40]

The victim mentality must be cast out just as much as the predator compulsion.

Two sides to fall off the track.

"So be careful to do what the The Maker has commanded you; do not turn aside to the right or to the left." Deuteronomy 5:32

The two sides of the menorah are counterfeited by predator and victim; too strict - too soft, too boxing in - too flexible with boundaries. Each of the seven lamps have their own strengths and weaknesses. The enemy comes to extinguish your personal flame. If he can't do that he will try to elevate it beyond the place The Maker has designed for you. Some of these gifts are elevated in certain cultures or circles and some despised, but all have their designated place.

The pride of the one who has been elevated I have heard called "balloon pride" while the pride of those who have been ignored or judged to be less useful (if useful at all - i.e.

---

[40] Terrible quote from: Sweet Dreams: Eurythmics

"I do not need you") could be called "worm pride" or "hurt pride".

"Every valley shall be exalted, and every mountain and hill shall be made low: and the crooked shall be made straight, and the rough places plain."
Isaiah 40:4

Some are built up too much and some need to be built up.

Some withdraw to a safe place, counting themselves out. Some dominate because they think they are doing better at representing The Maker. This is how the 'DNA damage' is done and another monster is created. We need all the parts. Who draws the circle to mark who is in and who is out? Who makes another feel like they are not part of the body? Who lets one dominate over another?

"people who *normally* get their way"

Though there are two sides to fall off the track, those who have retreated, withdrawn wounded and feeling outside the body, leave behind a diminished body: a monster. So eventually only those who are prone to say "We don't need you" are left. Those who are left will not be balanced by those who are gone.

Idolatry of another's flavour. Envy of another's flavour is rejection of the true self: your own flavour.

It has been a long tradition for those trying to be the body of messiah to make Frankensteinian monsters [41]. Like Frankenstein seeking to make the perfect person, we have

---

[41] Long before Mary Shelley wrote a word, 200 years ago.

made a million monsters. Parts of the body are missing or are deformed. Ignorance is not bliss. Even where these flavours are taught there is a long way to go because the group teaching it will have wider cultural prejudices and blind spots. Consciously or unconsciously when a person or group of people start a new group / denomination (do they have to?) they bring with them inherited distortions. They are usually in reaction to some fault they can see in the group they are leaving but don't know their own bias or other faults, which they have not seen and which they bring with them from the other group. I am not talking about doctrine here, though that too will be based on the elevated flavours' favourite verses and themes in Scripture, my aim is to point at the ethos. Much is said about doctrine, but without the context of Romans 12 diversity, so the dysfunction continues. When *a certain denomination,* for example, is filtering people through its colleges for its new leaders, they can't help but repeat the same pattern of elevating their own kind. It may be that they will let through a few who are differently flavoured from their version of the "alpha male" but how far or popular this difference would be allowed is limited. We naturally reproduce according to our kinds. It is even harder to watch this sort of thing happen to those who have already woken up to Torah and Israelite identity, not yet moving on to Romans chapter twelve. Pioneers are vulnerable to these unhelpful justifications of group identity, being so isolated. However, I do see good signs, tender shoots of beauty.

When people come with their ideas of: community, family, what is "normal", good etc, they come with their bias, their angle, their flavour. Unless they become aware of their bias they are bound to project onto others how they feel or what they think about another's words or actions. Without the wisdom of Romans chapter 12 we will project onto others our own strengths (not wise and potentially dangerous) and weaknesses (unproductive and judgmental). The harmonised body of Israel will not be mature in love without this key in Romans 12. It frees an individual to give room to another to be different.

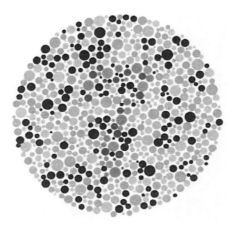

Denial of the differences = Prejudices in Romans 12 Diversity.

"For by the flavour(bias) given me, I say to every one of you: Do not think of yourself more highly than you ought, but rather think of yourself with sober judgment, in accordance with the faith The Maker has **distributed** to each of you." Romans 12:3(shared out)

In The Maker's great and wise love for people He did not pour all His attributes into one vessel. (Well actually He did in Messiah Yeshua of course! who is: "The visible expression of the invisible One"[42])

I have heard some say "we can become all of these". I answer that if we have not accepted our core gift and learnt of its strengths and weaknesses, we will not have a foundation for building on. We will be unfaithful to the gift we have and unaware of our bias. Surely we must establish what The Maker has given us before we rush off trying to be more. The health of one of our branches is dependent on having a healthy trunk.

When we are aware of these differences that exist in the body of messiah, we will become able to think about ourselves soberly. We will learn not to project our own strengths and weaknesses onto others or presume we understand when we don't. Though it is a process needing time, we will see the, "behold how beautiful it is when brethren dwell together in heavenly unity"[43].

"For just as each of us has one body with many members, and these members do not all have the same function, so in Messiah we, though many, form one body, and each member belongs to all the others. We have **different** gifts[44](favours / flavours), according to the grace given to each of us" Romans 12:4

To deny the differences is surely to
persecute the differences.

---

[42] Colossians 1:15 in the J.B.Phillips

[43] Psalm 133:1

[44] (χάρισμα charisma)

To start with, if we are not even able to name or recognise all the seven flavours, how could we possibly affirm them among us and therefore collectively reflect The Makers likeness? Without this humility we are bound to perpetuate the ugliness.

I write with my flavour's strengths and weaknesses. Can I speak for all mercy flavoured people in detail? No. But I trust I am voicing some of our common experience. My flavour's faults are on the victim or prey side of error. We are known more for flight than fight, especially when it comes to the need to confront error for example. We are often too quick to acknowledge our own weaknesses and bias. We are known for the frequency of use of the word "sorry" and for thinking we are guilty of something when we are not. But watch us when there is someone we think is being victimised and you will see no lack of power. I therefore write with boldness for the victim: The Maker's beautiful reflection in us. And with confidence to confront these Frankensteinian monsters which spread ugliness by blind prejudice. The will of man = Frankenstein Ambition.

No more monsters!

So to those who are challenged or offended by what I am fumbling to say, who am I? A broken servant who acknowledges that he is biased, perhaps even speaking partly from hurt. However I am someone who has the courage to go against his fears to dare to connect in a more meaningful way. Not to push anyone away. To have a good "fight" metaphorically speaking. I am asking to be trusted. Not to be totally right about what I am trying to say, but a voice of one crying in a wilderness   "It takes all seven to do this"! Meaning: Interdependence "I can't do this without you". I can't 'live' in hiding, nor do I want to be misunderstood as I make my attempts to connect. I risk. I am trying to vocalise something which I believe will bring riches beyond anything we have yet known. A vision beyond what we have seen so far, except for in shards and fragments.   A Key.

"Unless The Maker builds the house, the labourers labour in vain." Psalm 127:1

5 - The Bad News II

Some details of dysfunction

Let's go deeper, if you dare, into some details of our dysfunction. Acknowledging our bias, so that we can receive, like a child, the Kingdom in fullness.

When I heard this dynamite teaching, I thought surely everyone would want to know this but many do not. Perhaps it is a fear of being boxed too narrowly? Mistrust of yet another 'personality types' teaching? (This one *is* from The Maker! even if it can be twisted by people's blind spots). Other people's experience of this teaching has often been less dramatic than mine, for various reasons. Some have no trouble with accepting which gift they are, having been affirmed in it. Some just don't want their boat rocked, "If it ain't broke, don't fix it." Perhaps for them it does not seem an important message; however they may have inherited prejudices and attitudes that others feel acutely? Perhaps they fear the loss power and control?

For those of you who seem to be functioning fairly well.......I beseech you [45] mishpochah (family), to hear me out. Perhaps you have been affirmed by parent and environment alike. Good! That does not mean you are automatically able to be part of the body in a healthy way. Perhaps you have even been idolized or envied......that is not your fault. I am not able to write from your perspective. It is not my experience. I'll let you write about that. I am dependent on

---

[45] Romans12:1

you being hungry enough to be open to the bad news. We are inter-dependent.[46]

It is perhaps easier to see how ugly we have all been from my flavour's point of view, to receive the bad news. Harder to see it seems if your flavour has been elevated beyond design?

For me this teaching has given me room to exist. It has helped me stop trying to be something I simply am not. It helped me to recognise the sin of envy of another's flavour. It has freed me to accept others who are built differently but, more importantly, to accept my own flavour. I believe it has enabled me to love more maturely.

It is obvious that I was always this gift, looking throughout my childhood, even if I didn't become a believer until I was 20 years old. I only learnt about these flavours at 27 years old. I'm 52 now and I am still finding new understanding and beginning to see through more blind-spots I did not of course know I had. I have moved from the crude cartoon understanding I started with, to the less crude understanding I have now. As I said in the introduction, I have not found it easy to write this book, including all the bad news as I see it. I write vulnerably because I am seeking to remove specks from people's eyes, knowing that I am still learning about my own plank. Am I being foolish to try? I just know that I have reached a point where I feel I have little to lose and much to gain. This chapter is riskier because I am writing about something I experience personally which has been a source of wounding that may not yet be completely healed. I know that while I look to The

---

[46] Romans 14:7

Father of Lights I have confidence to write, though unfinished in healing.

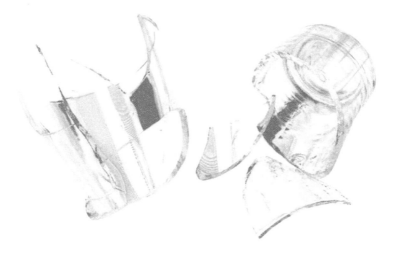

I am aware of some of my bias in writing this book. Please do not let my easy honesty of my own faults make you think I either see it all, or am blind to some of the faults of others. I trust that I am not motivated by bitterness or gripe. Instead by joyful confidence in The Maker's faithfulness to restore us, but only if we are honest about our brokenness.

So if, after this chapter, you feel compelled to help me remove the plank from my eye, please first check you are not projecting onto me sins I am not committing or motives I don't have. I welcome advice so long as it is with wisdom from above, knowing you are only one of these gifts at the core and therefore humble. I have had a lifetime of having faults projected onto me. I'm not going to take it lying down anymore! We do need one another to rebuke and encourage....but let us do this more wisely.

To the heart of the matter (from my perspective):

I frequently experience a form of 'flavourism' in many spheres of life. As with racism or sexism, it is communicated both verbally and non verbally. To talk about this is as dangerous as a walk in a minefield. I am not coming from a place of blame and attacking, though some flavours will be tempted to project that onto me, if they do not understand Romans 12 well.

An example of this 'flavourism' was when gathering with some believers recently. When I experienced it, I was therefore presented with a choice, to attempt to name the ugliness or to stay silent and let it pass: "let's pretend". I personally am easily triggered when the atmosphere seems to demand "Happy Families". I long for deep connections with these people who I have known for years, so I took the chance. Knowing that my flavour-tribe at their worst tend to express themselves either as a stormy emotional outburst or more usually as an inaudible whisper, when we are even a little anxious. I opened my mouth and spoke. I have no idea what I said but I could tell straight away that it was not going well. The response came fast and furious, "Don't you know that we love you?". I was dumb before the shearers. I would love to travel back in time to that moment and respond quickly "yes you do love me, but not with wise or mature love. I dared to challenge you because I thought you would hear me and because I care about all the others 'of my kind' who will feel the same lack of true acceptance from you." Instead I'm silent and after some despair I leave it in The Maker's capable hands. They don't seem ready to see the ugliness. But the thought buzzed about my head, "was it my fault?".

I don't enjoy the drama of confrontation......why? because of the disagreement? No. I don't mind a good fight...to voice differences. The reason is we are often not up for the fight.

The irony is that those who are usually the "strong people" now go all limp and turned into 'victims', hurt by what I have said! *They* withdraw! The same thing I do naturally....but they shouldn't (tongue in cheek ~ aware of lack of objectivity).

Historically they then encourage me to get more counselling for imagining prejudice, "bitter root judgement", rather than being willing to believe they could be in need of change. What price am I prepared to pay for this Kingdom of The Maker? How many people must I risk offending in the search for the health of the body? "People don't know how often I am letting pass this discrimination, deferring in the hope of change!" Mutter ... mutter.

Perhaps you experienced similar Romans12-ism or a different kind which Paul talks about[47]? That will change. It is changing. He promised.

It is as if this 'self-harm' in The Body has been decreed up till now as part of the curses for not listening and doing The Maker's instructions. When the enemy comes to us, we flee in seven different directions. The disunity is mostly when a 'group' dominates, even with the best of intentions, from ignorance of these seven differences Paul is teaching us. If we could all embrace our limits we would be ready to let The Maker "build the house".

"All animals are equal.
But some are more equal than others"[48]

---

[47] "don't need you" Corinthians

[48] George Orwell: Animal Farm

The Worldlings

I beseech you Mishpochah(family) .....don't be conformed to the pattern of this world[49]

Into the vacuum where Romans 12 wisdom should be, come: clingons, virgos, emos, phlegmatics, vulcans, elves, skaters, goths, empaths, wizards, Yoda types, X-men, ESTJs, Sagittarians, Alphas, etc etc etc etc

From Books to Film, from role play: Dungeons & Dragons, World of War Craft, Sim / Virtual worlds to man-made or 'enemy-made' religions, Scientology, come definitions of personalities and personality types till they are coming out of our ears. Unconscious and conscious attempts at explaining and enjoying the abundant diversity plainly seen round about us. Room for "Equality and Diversity" ad nauseum, yet never able to capture the rich wonder of Romans 12. How could they? Each of the story tellers are limited in their perspective. Limited not just by their unbelief in The Maker and His promises but also by their single core flavour. Romans 12 is all around us. However it is hidden from those who do not receive the revelation from The Maker of the menorah.

---

[49] Romans 12:2

Counterfeit rainbow fruits. Counterfeits of what?

Very often the believing world is so afraid of the counterfeits, such as star-signs, that we become afraid of the very real things which are being counterfeited or crudely copied. Through fear of their territory being rocked they resist the change that could bring richness and beauty back to us. If the counterfeits are a poor copy, let The Maker give us a glimpse of the Real we lost through rebellion.

The film Divergent is a story about a future society divided into five "factions" or categories. Here is a quote from one of the leaders to some young people on the special day they are choosing their "faction", "The Faction system is a living being composed of cells: all of you. And the only way it can survive and thrive, is for each of you to claim your rightful place. The future belongs to those who know where they belong." If they don't fit they become "factionless" outsiders / homeless. ~ I would be factionless in that society because my motivation is merged and distorted by the writer's unconscious bias. I wouldn't exist. Only five types, so two are missing or merged, ... another monster. ~ The sequel, Insurgent, is about the system falling apart because people not fitting or being more than one type. It is a story about how to be a 'corporate living being' / society, but humanistically. But we have Romans 12 (in context)! The basic message of these films, as I see it, is that because of war a system of dividing society into five separated groups is established: selfless, intelligent, brave, peaceful and honest,...but it isn't working because we don't fit that mould.

The main danger I see in the film is that "you can be what you want" - Ambition...the unsurrendered will. Two ways to swing off The Maker's way, by boxing people in ignorance and in false ways, or by telling people they are free from The Maker's wise limitations, i.e of having one at the core. Fun film though.

~

Where a richly diverse expression of The Maker, reflected in Israel, is missing, the world does its best to grapple crudely with difference. The world ropes gender brokenness and other perversions into the eclectic spectrum of life and that won't work. The world throws the baby out with the bath water of churchy narrowness.

Sometimes the "worldlings", free from inherent traditional distortions of scripture, are able, if we listen to them, to open our eyes to something we may have lost on the way. They see the dominance of certain gifts which then become comically characterised. Perhaps Spock for example, is one character which needed to appear in popular culture because of the elevation of reason and logic over emotion and imagination?

Rhyme and Reason

This cartoon is shown to many new believers in large parts of Christendom to this day. There are a few versions but emotion is always the last carriage!

You say, 'I am rich; I have acquired wealth and do not need a thing.' But you do not realise that you are wretched, pitiful, poor, blind and naked.
Revelation 3:17

It is one thing to experience tension due to our different focuses and abilities when it is one to one, but to enter into a group environment that claims to have a monopoly of the image of The Maker and teaching the above, is life threatening for some of us on the Romans 12 list. Not that this cartoon, on its own, could do much but a whole paradigm will.

Room for reasons in military order, at the ready.
But Rhymes are kept in dusty boxes, stifled
and forgotten at the back of cupboards.
Reasons travel in lines: slicing, dicing, analysing.
Restored, rhymes dance out word combinations that

unlock untried doors and win great battles.

Divorced to cease the strife.

Together again, a powerful couple.

I was already very damaged goods when I became a believer: Family, school ing, and general 1960 / 70's British culture taught me this same idea, "Stiff upper lip" linked to "I know a man by his grip". Boys who were emotional, were seen as weak or homosexual. Since then a quantum shift has taken place bulldozing gender stereotypes but not solving all the problems. Try doing a google search for the word Empath for example. It seems Mercy people are finding a voice[50]. The resistant diehard evangelical alpha male holds on to his tradition not knowing that it is a monster, even though we have had characters like Mr Spock to laugh at for his extremely cold logic. It is not just culture led by those who are more vulcan, but those with them, who have bought into that spirit.

In many Christian circles this enemy inspired cartoon is taught as truth. I am indebted and in awe of those who are built a little like Spock. Nobody wants to remove those who are teacher flavoured or prophet flavoured, or any other gift who can hide or control their emotions easily. If people understood Empath-Mercy types, they would know that we forgive easily (once we see that we need to!) and we have no desire to take over the universe, replacing one swing towards cold logic with another where all that is valued is a sea of emotion.

---

[50] This search will show that being empathetic is very different to being an empath.

Once when I shared a tiny amount of my struggles with gender identity, I was given a book: "Maximised manhood"! It was seeking to define a biblical man. Oy Vey! I found it alienating and ignorant of the diversity in The Maker.

How many times should we forgive?[51] Seven? 70 x 7

Even when I was first taught about Romans 12 there was advice given to the mercy motivated to be balanced by others due to their emotions. As a mercy I received that wisdom simply. However it registered emotionally inside somewhere that that advice was not given to the less obviously emotional people on the list, needing to be balanced with more the emotional ones. This general fear of emotion or demoting of emotion, means that the "empath" is feared when being free to be themselves in some circles. Emotions are not trustworthy but logic is? Think again. Once this rejection is experienced, it is hard to be "objective".

The evangelical view of man, particularly, nearly killed me. But now I have room to see man through new, wider and wilder eyes. The spice of creativity and sweet feelings finally have their place in my exploratory 'man-ness'. No slugs or snails or puppy dog's tails required.

If I no longer experienced all this I would not mention it. An appeal to my fellow pioneering returnees to Torah and Israelite identity: please jettison this dark baggage of elevating the intellect over emotion. Looking back with this understanding I was able to see how the people I became a believer through at the age of twenty, could not accept me and wanted me to be something else. They did not know of

---

[51] Matthew 18:21

Romans 12 in this way and they therefore constantly tried to change me.

His Kingdom come His will be done! An end to this misrepresentation of The Maker! "Do not be conformed to pattern[52] of this world: but be transformed by the renewing of your mind, that you may prove what *is* that good, and acceptable, and perfect, will of The Maker" Romans12:2. No more prideful distortions in the name of Messiah. Even the "world" seems to value emotion better!

"Foolish things of the world to shame that which is wise."[53]

"Not by might not by power but by my Ruach(Spirit) says The Maker."[54]

EXPLAIN YOURSELF!

Countless times I have faced a demand for an immediate explanation which if I do not give within a second, results in that triumphant facial expression and an exhale of victory: "Humph!....I thought so......you can't, can you!" Meaning that I am either lying, hiding something, unsure, evasive, or at best untrustworthy. Of course this becomes cyclic. 'Guilty' of not being like those who are able to respond quickly leads to feelings of failure, which make explanation even more unattainable. "Cat got your tongue?" Without the key of Romans 12 taught well, what alternative but to retreat and wait for change? When we do retreat it is seen as cowardice or judgementalism.

---

[52] Exodus 25:9 & 40

[53] 1Corinthians 1:27

[54] Zechariah 4:6

However let me try and *explain* the foolishness of the train illustration: This attempt to help people come closer to The Maker, by teaching that the 'facts' of scripture are what we need so as to be free, "the truth will set you free", is faulty logic. It misunderstands how we diversely receive truth. For the Mercy flavoured, emotion is the foundational way we find out what can be trusted. This form of knowing is emotional. In English we have just the one word: knowing, while in French we have two words for knowing: 'connaitre' which is knowing a person and in contrast: 'savoir' which is about knowing details and information. This can help explain the type of knowledge the Mercy flavour experiences easily and is dependent on having confidence in.

Even intense feelings of grief, depression and rejection are essential and valuable to ensure health in the long term. The illustration communicates an untrustworthiness of feelings, but thoughts and reasoning are damaged too in us broken people, and to suggest emotions are less trustworthy than thought and reason, is not helpful or true. Blindness is blindness and we need a miracle to change the situation. So at best this illustration confuses knowing with details and analytical knowledge only and at worst it rejects a whole breed of individuals. Mercy logic is less easily explainable or put into words. (Arthur Burk says that the first six flavours are like PCs and the Mercy flavoured are like Apple Macs.[55])

The Big fact is that The Maker loves us.....will you feel that love if you are blocked? Not easily. Both your thoughts and feelings need to be heard. The fact of His love, believed

---

[55] www.youtube.com/watch?v=bRgpBniBycQ (6 minutes in)

despite bad experiences, does come first. Learning this fact deeply will be through an encounter with that Love. The way through to intimacy with The Maker is having the courage to travel through all the thoughts and feelings until they have been absorbed by His powerful love. This takes time. The almost inevitable message the illustration conveys is that reason and logic will save you (you will save yourself) and those feelings will change with time even *if you don't dare to face them with The Maker!* To ignore the gift of negative emotion is to ignore the path to Love. So if you feel awful, there's a good reason for it!

"Taste and see that The Maker is good; blessed is the one who takes refuge in him."[56]

Apparently receiving the Kingdom as a little child is evil!?

Due to the reasoning and logical flavours being elevated in various circles, knowledge has often become controlled in an occultic kind of way. Knowledge of prophecy, cosmology, the supernatural, deep stuff, has been allowed to be studied and taught at the same time as not seeing how far we have strayed from The Maker's basic instructions.

Much of what is written in the 'New Testament' is on a Kabbala level from a Jewish perspective. It may be seen as erroneous or dodgy but on the Kabbalistic level none the less. Sadly the ethos of the evangelical world is generally condemning of the word Kabbala (*to receive* in Hebrew - LeKabel / קָבַל) and anything *they* think is Kabbalistic, while

---

[56] Psalm 34:8

ironically focussing on extensive conspiratorial knowledge of evil counterfeits, false deities, hollywood occult imagery, illuminati symbolism….all in an extremely obsessive occult-like way. Holding to all sorts of deep ideas of the 'New Testament', while not 'receiving' the basic instructions and narrative of the 'Old Testament' looks to me like occult-ist behaviour! Every time someone says that Kabbala is evil, another Mercy falls to the ground!! Into the vacuum of true knowledge of our diversity, (how wonderfully we have been made!) come monstrous disease and disorder. The landscapes of the heart are mapped out simply enough in The Maker's Instructions (laws, commandments), which are ignored because we are in 'new' era?! Rejecting these maps, leaves us listening to the strongest voices while wandering in the wilderness. So receiving (in hebrew: Kabbala) like a child, which a Mercy type person is naturally able to do well, is <u>not</u> a bad thing. We must avoid the occult. Let us listen diligently to our Master to avoid it.

The solution: "Would a good Father give a stone instead of bread?"[57]

To receive amazing truth in an 'intuitive' way is fine and good. Yes, it has to somehow fit the main narrative of Scripture but not with the test of people who have fearful control of doctrine. Fear always diminishes, kills, blinds and misses the best.

---

[57]Matthew 7:9

This is not a comprehensive dispassionate fault finding analysis. It is a heartfelt, passionate personal perception of my experience in The Body. Therefore I know very well that I'm blind to many areas of disfunction that may be crying out to you. I have stared at the screen for hours wondering what is missing in these two bad-news chapters. As if we want any more bad news! If I have stirred in you the awareness of how both the good tension in diversity and the ugly disfunction around us, are allowed by The Maker to lead us to hunger for more, then I have succeeded!

~

For your prayer and perhaps empathy, I want to share a challenge we face as a family. I could talk about my dramatic, challenging encounters with prophet flavoured ones who I am naturally attracted to for their clarity, but who I feel at times like locking up to keep away from someone they may harm. Or about Servers who feel safe to me but who I remain in awe of practically. Or with teacher shaped people who have driven me crazy with their need for loads of detail that I simply can't give them. Or Encouragers with the confusion I have felt about how present they feel and yet they tend to put an Elastoplast on wounds that need major surgery. Or Organisers who have remained a distant reality, yet to be known deeply. Instead I want to share about our experience in relating to two of our children who we think are Givers. (both my wife and I, are Mercy flavoured)

According to Andy's book where he talks about couple combinations, he writes that a Mercy-Giver couple is a peaceful safe place for hospitality and a haven for wounded people. Well we have a different experience of being close to Givers! We do have Giver friends who we enjoy and value. I learnt about the seven flavours at least three years before our eldest son was born but we were unable to recognise, let alone affirm, his gifting before he left our house a few years ago. We thought perhaps he must be Mercy or Organiser, but never felt clear and we were confused. It is painful to see how The Maker has allowed this time of ignorance and disfunction to get in the way of a comfortable connection.

We did not know, while he was with us, that both my wife and I had a particular blindspot to do with Giver shaped people. The Maker chose to use this blindspot, giving us two children who we found hard to recognise. Very soon after our son left us in an unpleasant kind of way, "our eyes were opened" (~ we think): both the eldest son and the second daughter are Giver flavoured. The tension between the Mercy and the Giver flavours is 'interesting' and painful. So knowing about these things will lead to mistakes and humbling. We are limited. Knowing your weakness is good and sobering. But we are learning that the tension comes when both of us as parents who are built to laugh and cry with people, have a child (or two) who are very independent emotionally. What a mystery!

With this blind spot of this area of the heavenly spectrum, both me and my wife, with siblings who are Giver motivated, missed years of pleasant unity (even with tension) with these two in our home. We are still needing to learn about how to live with the Mercy / Giver close relationships, especially because one of them is still with us. Quite some tension! We are comforted by the verse: "all things work together for good to them that love The Maker, to those who are the called according to his purpose"[58] We share this to caution against thinking that all blindspots disappear when you have studied the information about Romans 12.

I have a passion for beauty and an ugly habit of not trusting Abba[59].

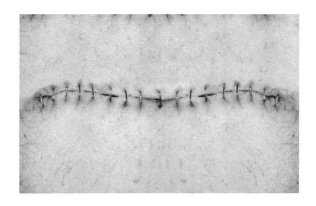

"I believe! help my unbelief"

Proverbs 6:16-18 "These six things The Maker hates: yes, seven are an abomination to him: A proud look, a lying tongue, and hands that shed innocent blood, a heart that devises wicked imaginations, feet that be swift in running to mischief, a false witness that speaks lies, and he that sows discord among brethren.

---

[58] Romans 8:28

[59]Father in The Heavens

~

Seven divergent roads, a curse fulfilled.
Seven languages, discord as at Babel.
Seven severed bleeding body parts.
Some sewn together in strange design.
Suffering transplant rejection.
Some cast off as alien:
"You don't fit in" "You're odd" "I do not need you"
Another silly idol.
Another humanistic monster.
Always claiming to please The Maker.
Blind guides take their turn, all stumble.
Nation robbed of cohesion, marring The Face we are to mirror.
But One only, worthy to open the seal.
Those grieving for the divided house are with Him.
Waiting.
One Beautiful Bride.

Time for "I did it His way" instead of "I did it my way".
That's the bad news out of the way. Can you feel the good news coming?

6 - The good news is: You are beautiful!

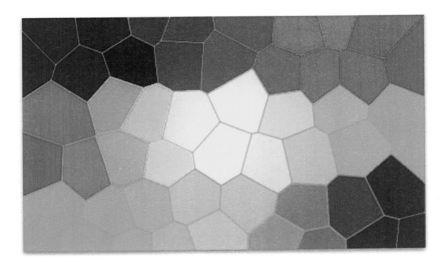

You are a beautiful body of different parts,
held in perfect tension.
Extremities and a core,
seamlessly knit into a harmony of multifunction.
Hard bone and supple flesh.
Inside and out: beyond analysis.
Too wonderful for words.
To be used by Him or laid aside from service.
Room for the contrasting voices.
Rhyme and Reason. Dance and Harvest.
Steeled for war and intimate touch.
Full of the word of life.
Healthy and Strong.
You are beautiful.
Am Yisrael Chai!
(People of Israel Live!)

The Yovel Year is near (Jubilee Year).

Let the promised resurrection of your beauty complete. Israel will be that beautiful bride as He said. Then will His instructions, words of eternal life, flow from our capital, Jerusalem, just as fresh water will flow into the 'dead' sea and teem with life. The whole earth waits for this: The Good news.

Gathering now in small clusters of Israelite cells, humbled, we can learn of our limits to our expression of that Unlimited One. Romans 12 Wise love replacing both fight and flight, in preparation to be taken home to the land. In sober contrition we will "stand firm and see the rescue of The Maker"[60], for He is determined to restore His image here on earth. Tikkun (repair) is not a question of our ambition but of His faithful promise. His doing. It will happen. Coming whether you are ready or not.

The tension between each of these very different gifts is essential to our unity. It seems obvious that people have fallen out over doctrine and practice, but it is less obvious or even invisible to those who don't yet understand Romans 12, that many of the ugly attacks or retreats are about insecurity in these gift / flavour differences. I have watched people calling for unity by not falling out over doctrine yet these same people have directly caused division by making a declaration about something not all the flavours can agree to. They are not yet aware of their inherent bias. It is so painful to watch this gagging of a gift in the name of 'all'. So The Maker wills that we learn about these gifts in Romans

---

[60] Exodus 14:13 Deuteronomy 30 ....

12 to free us from this vicious cycle. He is opening this wisdom up that we may be whole.

We do not focus on our weaknesses but on The Painter as He chooses from His palette. Now this colour and now that colour. Let Him be King of Light.

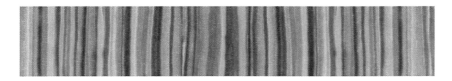

For now it is simple trust, not seeing, not being overwhelmed by ugliness. Overcoming ugliness with beauty. Covering one another's weaknesses and affirming each other's gifts. Time for one, time for another.

A land with: wheat and barley, vines and fig trees, pomegranates, olive oil and date honey.[61]

"And YHWH passed by before him, and proclaimed, YHWH, YHWH El merciful and gracious, longsuffering, and abundant in goodness and truth, keeping mercy for thousands, forgiving iniquity and transgression and sin, and that will by no means clear *the guilty*; visiting the iniquity of the fathers upon the children, and upon the children's children, till the third and to the fourth *generation*."[62]

---

[61] Deuteronomy 8:8

[62] Exodus 34:6-7

The beauty of The Maker is in the perfect tension between All His Attributes.[63]

Divided into 7, yet a rainbow spectrum. Here on earth there is a line between each flavour, yet in the Maker, it is a spectrum[64] with no division: seamless.

Seven congregations with wisdom to each in the book of Revelation: Ephesus, Smyrna, Pergamos, Thyatira, Sardis, Philadelphia, and Laodicea.
One nation in exile.

"I will plant in the wilderness the cedar, the shittah tree, and the myrtle, and the oil tree; I will set in the desert the fir tree, and the pine, and the box tree together"[65]

We are branches on the menorah tree of life. We must be conformed into His image and no longer conformed to the Frankenstein monsters, man-made distortions.

These gifts are not too small, they are generously rich. You are not being boxed, but freed to celebrate the wonder of the advantage He has planted in you.

"Wisdom has built her house, she has hewn out her seven pillars"[66]
Another good picture. Pillars which together are able to create a safe space to shelter many. It would not do to have

---

[63] Isaiah 11:2

[64] Ezekiel 1:28

[65] Isaiah 41:19

[66] Proverbs 9:1

the pillars too far apart to avoid tension or too close to avoid tension; we need the tension to create the space.

The words of The Maker are pure words: as silver tried in a furnace of earth, purified seven times. Psalms 12:6

Listen to advice and receive[67] discipline, and at the end you will be counted among the wise. Proverbs 19:20

The seven days of the week. Wise order to give a good rhythm to life. Work, Rest and Pray (and Play).

While it is true that where two or three are gathered together in His name, there He will be with us, perhaps only when all seven flavours are present can we truly hear a more complete sound of the heavenly orchestra?

Furniture in the Mishkan(tent of meeting): Altar of Burnt Offering, Laver, Table of Showbread, The Lampstand, Altar of Incense, Ark of the covenant, Mercy seat. (At Beitel where the Mishcan was for a while I heard someone teaching about how there are only six pieces of furniture in the Mishcan.........guess which one was missing from his list: Mercy seat!). It was when all the furniture of the Mishcan were put in order and dedicated that The Presence came down.

---

[67] LeKabel - קָבַל

Photo (Xenopeltis - Sunbeam Snake) by Elissa Wilson

Wise as serpents - Harmless as doves

I once saw a video of the knitting together of a baby in the first stages of development. It was stunning. It really looked like knitting in action. I noticed that two shapes would form next to each other for a time and then it looked like they separated and joined other parts in a kind of dance. It is not instinctive, it seems, for us to move away from a group or individuals. It seems like division or schism but it is not always, nor need it be. The Maker's higher wisdom. He is knitting. It is sometimes that relationships are for a season. Only when we fight this wisdom in insecurity is there discord and distortion. Each part listening.

"The Lamb had seven horns and seven eyes, which are the seven spirits of The Maker sent out into all the earth."[68]

"We are His bride taken from His side,
when blood and water fell
from the broken heart of Israel.
See YHWH provide, the precious lamb who died.
The great I Am who cried,
"Eli Eli lama sabachtani"[69].
Abba.
El Shaddai.
To The Maker I give my life."
-
"And we being many are one body, in messiah.
And everyone members of one another.
Loving each other with El as our Father,
who loves us as a mother loves her new-born child."[70]

We will "discern the body" [71] with its extremes and its balance. Not a dumb grey homogenised gloop. Motivational flames burning bright. Our high essences, a pleasing aroma. Orderly service in every sphere. Blessing instead of the curses.

Variety is the spice of life.

---

[68] Revelation 5:6 Zechariah 3:9 & 4:10

[69] My El, My El, why have you abandoned me?

[70] Words from 'Nothing but the Best' - Helen Shapiro.

[71] 1Corinthians 11:29

So, let your flavour flood out….

….and we will soon:
"Sing and be glad on the heights of Zion"[72]

---

[72] Jeremiah 31:12

7 - Conclusion

"Come, let us return to The Maker. He has torn us to pieces but He will heal us; He has injured us but He will bind up our wounds." Hosea 6:1

Romans 12 is wisdom to love maturely. We have various differences: male and female, various educational and wealth backgrounds, a spectrum of experience with insecure to secure childhoods, etc, yet Romans 12, if you can *receive* it, will open up rich differences that enable us to reflect the full image of The Invisible One.

When Israel and all those who came out with us, becoming Israel too, left Egypt in the first exodus, we were called into a role of reflecting The Maker's image to the other nations. When we "drink the blood" and "eat the body" of Yeshua the 'lamb' at passover, we are strengthened to leave an inner Egypt of slavery to go to a new place of fullness of life, beginning to receive Torah deep down in the heart. In the Greater Exodus to come All Israel will be rescued from among the nations and brought home to the land of Israel for the 'The Great Shabbat': A thousand years of "His will be done on Earth".

How do we walk out these covenant relationships at this time? We do not need others to recognise our flavour to be able to be in covenant relationship with them. We can not be told who we are or where we should be, by another part of the body. The Maker alone tells each of us who we are and where our place is. Only by forgiving as we have been forgiven and loving as we have been loved, can we walk this way. However when we recognise the flavour in each other we will be open to being knit together in The Maker's perfect timing and design.

I claim that this teaching has brought me much light and encouragement to persevere with people I would have probably given up on long ago. I am also learning that there is a time to resist and refuse submission to unhealthy and immature attempts at defining The house of Israel,The Body,The Menorah. To define who is 'us' and who is not 'us' or who is 'in' and who is 'out' must not be done in insecurity or ignorance of Romans12. In the fear of The Maker let us hold back from the well worn path of *congregation making* without the foundational keys of Israelite National identity and Romans 12 diversity and Torah / Heavenly Instructions and much <u>humility</u>.

"Therefore, I beseech you brethren, that you present yourselves sacrificially." Romans 12:1

Just because we may think we have got away with making monsters, doesn't mean we have not sown a harvest of trouble yet to appear. Do not confuse The Maker's long suffering with weakness.

Romans chapter 13 verse 1 moves us on to "the governing authorities". Who these are is disputed, but see how we have first resolved "who we are" in chapter 12, before we head into authority structures. The jobs and tools are only able to work well when the gifts of Romans 12 are understood humbly. The rest of the book of Romans calls for patience and kindness with all.

So let us hold posture, not rushing into declarations of group identity in the tradition of those who have gone before. Let us humbly learn about and give room for, the full spectrum in Joseph's coat, and when we think it absolutely necessary to make statements and define, that we do it with much caution and a listening ear to *all* the voices, not missing any flavours out. Remember some of the voices take time to be heard. Then our identity will grow from security in Him and we will produce nothing but good fruit. This starts with one, then with a couple and a family, all within the Nation of Israel.

This is difficult as so many of us are isolated in this pioneering. Truly we were torn to pieces. How we come together is critical. His timing will mean something beautiful. Let The Maker guide, knit, and form us. How many times have hands been sown to heads or feet to arms? How many times have Servers, Givers or others, been used and abused just to achieve some good-looking goal? Or a stuttering voice challenging, judged as decent or rebellion? Congregational identity is a horrible history of cancerous monstrosity.

Fear cannot define us. In awe of Him and lost in wonder, let us listen for His life-giving voice beyond our knowledge and our wisdom. Let us not fall to the temptation to explain our position. Let us tussle, fight, grapple, face these issues……..no more cutting off parts of the body in His Name. No more slipping into the ways of ordering the body which abuse people. No more trying to fit where we do not fit. Let us learn to live with the tension there is between these gifts.

If we can not yet agree then we must leave it open until perhaps a time when we can see a way. Perhaps it is the same as when the slower sheep in the first exodus were at the back. Let us not close the circle, excluding the 'stragglers' as we perceive them by rushing ahead.

Love One Another……as I have loved you.
Yeshua is the Menorah Rainbow of Light, the full expression of the invisible One.
(Author and Finisher of our trust)

"I in the them, and You in me - so that they may be brought to complete unity. Then the world will know that you sent me and have loved them as You have loved me." John 17:23

"Behold, how good and how pleasant it is for brethren to dwell together in unity!" Psalm 133:1

"Let your people come together in unity...What a blessing He's commanding. When we are together the oil is flowing, descending from the heavens like the morning dew, pouring on our heads precious oil from you. Falling from the mountain, water fresh and cool.....Running down the beard and we know it's true. How pleasant, how good, how beautiful it is."[73]

---

[73] Selah Music, by James Block

Appendix

The front cover obviously has the spectrum of colour and hints at the spectrum of texture with the smooth colour gradient and the wonderfully bumpy skin of the Chameleon. The Chameleon is used ambiguously because if you have read my first book "A Skeleton in the room and Elephant in the closet" you will know how much I love them. However they have a monstrous quality don't you think?

- Andy Raine: "Given For Life. A guide to motivational gifts."

- Jackson Snyder: www.jacksonsnyder.com/mgi/

- Arthur Burk: Sapphire Leadership Group / Plumbline Ministries

www.theslg.com/content/131-redemptive-gifts-of-individuals-introduction

He also teaches about seven curses on Israel which need to be broken and the blessings that replace them.

www.theslg.com/content/124-curses-and-blessings

- James Block: Selah Music

www.shalomyisrael.com

- Bill Gothard:

www.iblp.org/questions/what-are-seven-motivational-gifts

Composite Names of The Maker:

- *YHWH-Yireh* — will Provide (<u>Genesis 22:13–14</u>)
- *YHWH-Rapha* — that Heals (<u>Exodus 15:26</u>)
- *YHWH-Niss"i* — our Banner (<u>Exodus 17:8–15</u>)
- *YHWH-Shalom* — our Peace (<u>Judges 6:24</u>)
- *YHWH-Ro'i* — my Shepherd (Psalm 23)
- *YHWH-Tsidkenu* — our Righteousness (<u>Jeremiah 23:6</u>)
- *YHWH-Shammah* — is Present (<u>Ezekiel 48:35</u>)

"Seven nations greater and mightier than you"…cast out before us:

Hittites, Girgashites, Amorites, Canaanites, Perizzites, Hivites, Jebusites,

The Second Greater Exodus:

Deuteronomy 30:1–10

Jeremiah 23:7 "So then, the days are coming," declares YHWH, "when people will no longer say, 'As surely as YHWH lives, who brought the Israelites up out of Egypt,' but they will say, 'As surely as YHWH lives, who brought the descendants of Israel up out of the land of the north and out of all the countries where he had banished them.' Then they will live in their own land." (and verse 8)

Isaiah 10:20, 11:11&16
Jeremiah 16:14 >15
Jeremiah 31:20 > 32
Hosea 1:10–11 Both houses gathered together.
Hosea 5:15 > 6:2 till they admit their guilt
Hosea 8:10
Hosea 11:10,11 He will roar
Hosea 13:14 Delivered from death
Amos 9:8–15
Obadiyah 18 and Zechariah 9:13
Both joined to fight against Edom.